the day i was CONFIRMED

Pam Lucas

Hal Harrison

the day i was CONFIRMED

United Church Press

Cleveland, Ohio

United Church Press, Cleveland, Ohio 44115

Printed in Hong Kong on acid-free paper

03 02 01 00 99 98   5 4 3 2 1

ISBN 0-8298-1280-6

the day i was CONFIRMED

THIS BOOK IS PRESENTED TO

(name)

ON THE DAY OF YOUR CONFIRMATION

BY

(name of church)

ON

(date)

(minister)

(representative of the congregation)

To the Minister and the Church:

This book is designed to help young people connect their Confirmation to their Baptism.

We hope that this book will help them reflect on the story of their faith journey, remind them of the importance of the promises they make on this occasion, and connect for the young person the relationship between Baptism, Confirmation, and lifelong discipleship.

You can help tell this story by:

- Encouraging the parent(s)/guardian(s) to recall the information about the child's Baptism and provide a picture for page 3.
- Inserting photos of your church exterior and interior and your minister on pages 4, 7, and 8.
- Providing a copy of the Confirmation questions as a reference for page 9.
- Filling in the words that are spoken at the time of Confirmation on page 10.
- Providing a way for additional photos of the young person, the family and friends, the sponsors or mentors, and the congregation to be taken on the day of Confirmation.
- Writing about the church's hopes for the one confirmed on page 12.
- Encouraging the parent(s)/guardian(s) to write personal words of hope on page 12.

To the Confirmand:

Confirmation is one of the most important days in your life. You have grown to the point where you are able to take responsibility for what you believe. This book will become your remembrance of this time.

When you are confirmed, you complete the sacrament of Baptism, because Baptism is not complete until *you* have confirmed it. In Baptism you were touched with the flame of God's Spirit upon your soul. Your parents and the church have been carefully tending that flame until this day when you can say for yourself, "I believe!" (If you were not baptized as a child, you will be baptized as part of your Confirmation.)

Just as Confirmation completes Baptism, we are asking you to complete this book. Part of it is a reflection on your past journey of faith, and part is a record and a reflection on your day of Confirmation. Ask your parent(s)/guardian(s) and your minister to help you get the photos and the copies of the service pieces that are needed to make this *your* book.

As you prepare for Confirmation, take some time to think about the questions on pages 1 and 2 and record your thoughts. Perhaps you will do them as a part of your Confirmation class.

You can fill in some of the details and pictures before your day of Confirmation. In the week after your day of Confirmation, you can finish your book.

"This is the covenant that I will make. . . . I will put my law within them, and I will write it on their hearts; and I will be their God, and they shall be my people."

—Jeremiah 31:33

confirmed

myself

Who are you?

List words that describe yourself.

Physically

Mentally

Spiritually

Physically

Mentally

Spiritually

What did you think about God when you were very little?

What do you believe about God now?

What do you still wonder about?

What do you still want to learn about?

This is what I looked like when I was ___*(at the age of Baptism)*___.

[insert picture]

That's how old I was when I was baptized.

The date was ______________________.

The name of the church was ______________________.

It was in ___*(name of town)*___.

My parent(s)/guardian(s) have helped me to grow up into Christian faith and discipleship. The whole church has been teaching me what it means to love God and to be a Christian. Now I am ready to tell the church that I want to live my life as a disciple of Jesus. On the day I was confirmed, I went to ______________________________ *(name of church)*.

[insert picture of church exterior]

I want to live my life as a disciple of Jesus.

The date was ____.

The weather was ____.

And I was ________ years old.

[insert picture of yourself on the day of Confirmation]

Some other people who loved me came with me:

Some of my friends in the church are:

[insert picture of family and friends]

There were other people at church that day. The church is a place where people come to

When it was time for me to be confirmed, I came forward to this place.

[insert picture of church interior]

The minister who confirmed me was ____.

[insert picture of minister]

The minister talked about my Baptism. I believe Baptism is ____________________

____

____

The minister talked about what it has meant to grow up in the church. Some of the people who have been important to me in the church are:

They have helped me by:

The minister asked me these questions:

The minister asked God to help me keep my promises. My prayer on this day is:

I knelt to be confirmed. The minister placed hands upon my head and said:

____

____

____

____

During my Confirmation, I felt ______________________________

____

____

Other things that happened during the service were [songs, gifts, symbols, etc.]:

____

____

____

Being a member of the church means

____

____

____

[insert picture of members of the congregation]

Being a disciple of Jesus Christ means:

____

____

____

Loving God with all my heart, mind, soul, and strength for the rest of my life means:

____

____

____

My church's hopes and prayers for me on the day of my Confirmation:

____

____

____

____

____

What my parent(s)/guardian(s) hope and pray for me on the day of my Confirmation:

____

____

____

____

____

"Let me tell you my story."

Now when someone asks me, "What is Confirmation?" I can say, "Let me tell you my story." And I can share with them this book. The journey of faith will continue in all the places I go.